Your first 100 words in

GREEK

Beginner's Quick & Easy Guide to Demystifying Greek Script

Series concept
Jane Wightwick

Illustrations
Mahmoud Gaafar

Greek edition
Ioanna Psalti

PASSPORT BOOKS
NTC/Contemporary Publishing Group

Other titles in this series:

Your First 100 Words in Arabic
Your First 100 Words in Chinese
Your First 100 Words in Hebrew
Your First 100 Words in Japanese
Your First 100 Words in Korean
Your First 100 Words in Russian

Cover design by Nick Panos

Published by Passport Books
A division of NTC/Contemporary Publishing Group, Inc.
4255 West Touhy Avenue, Lincolnwood (Chicago), Illinois 60712-1975 U.S.A.
Copyright © 2001 by Gaafar & Wightwick
Printed in the United States of America
International Standard Book Number: 0-658-01139-1
3 4 5 6 7 8 9 0 VLP VLP 0 5 4 3

⊙ CONTENTS

⊚ INTRODUCTION

In this activity book you'll find 100 key words for you to learn to read in Greek. All of the activities are designed specifically for reading non-Latin script languages. Many of the activities are inspired by the kind of games used to teach children to read their own language: flashcards, matching games, memory games, joining exercises, etc. This is not only a more effective method of learning to read a new script, but also much more fun.

We've included a **Scriptbreaker** to get you started. This is a friendly introduction to the Greek script that will give you tips on how to remember the letters.

Then you can move on to the 8 **Topics**. Each topic presents essential words in large type. There is also a pronunciation guide so you know how to say the words. These words are also featured in the tear-out **Flashcard** section at the back of the book. When you've mastered the words, you can go on to try out the activities and games for that topic.

There's also a **Round-up** section to review all your new words and the **Answers** to all the activities to check yourself.

Follow this 4-step plan for maximum success:

1 Have a look at the key topic words with their pictures. Then tear out the flashcards and shuffle them. Put them Greek side up. Try to remember what the word means and turn the card over to check with the English. When you can do this, cover the pronunciation and try to say the word and remember the meaning by looking at the Greek script only.

2 Put the cards English side up and try to say the Greek word. Try the cards again each day both ways around. (When you can remember a card for 7 days in a row, you can file it!)

3 Try out the activities and games for each topic. This will reinforce your recognition of the key words.

4 After you have covered all the topics, you can try the activities in the Round-up section to test your knowledge of all the Greek words in the book. You can also try shuffling all the flashcards together to see how many you can remember.

This flexible and fun way of reading your first words in Greek should give you a head start whether you're learning at home or in a group.

⊚ SCRIPTBREAKER

The purpose of this Scriptbreaker is to introduce you to the Greek script and how it is formed. You should not try to memorize the alphabet at this stage, nor try to write the letters yourself. Instead, have a quick look through this section and then move on to the topics, glancing back if you want to work out the letters in a particular word. Remember, though, that recognizing the whole shape of the word in an unfamiliar script is just as important as knowing how it is made up. Using this method you will have a much more instinctive recall of vocabulary and will gain the confidence to expand your knowledge in other directions.

The Greek script is not nearly as difficult as it might seem at first glance. There are many letters that are the same as the English ones, there are capital letters, and, unlike English, words are usually spelled as they sound:

- Greek spelling and pronunciation are much more systematic than in English
- You will recognize some of the letters straight away, but beware of false friends!

⊚ The alphabet

There are 24 letters in the Greek alphabet. A good way of learning the alphabet is to take it in three stages.

Stage 1

The first group consists of 10 letters which look and sound like their English equivalents – but watch out for lower case Z (ζ) and M (μ).

The first 8 are :

Capital letter:	A	E	Z	I	K	M	O	T
Lower case:	α	ε	ζ	ι	κ	μ	ο	τ
Pronunciation:	*a*	*e*	*z*	*i*	*k*	*m*	*o*	*t*

The next two letters are misleading as they resemble English letters but are not exact equivalents:

Capital letter:	N	Y
Lower case:	ν	υ
Pronunciation:	*n*	*i*

We can now use these letters to make a word:

μάτι   _mati_   eye

✔ Greek has 24 letters
✔ Some letters are like their English equivalents
✔ Some letters look like their English equivalents, but are **false friends**

Stage 2

This stage consists of letters which resemble the English letters as capitals and/or lower case but they are tricky as they represent totally different sounds. These are called "false friends."

Capital letter:	B	H	P	X
Lower case:	β	η	ρ	χ
Pronunciation:	v	i	r	h (hard)

We can use these letters to make some more words

χέρι   _heri_   hand

μικρό   _mikro_   small

μύτη   _miti_   nose

✔ There are four false friends:
B, β = v   H, η = i   P, ρ = r   X, χ = h

Stage 3

Here you will find all the letters which have unfamiliar shapes, although most of them represent sounds familiar to an English-speaker.

The first four letters represent sounds which in English are made by putting two letters together.

Capital letter:	Δ	Θ	Ξ	Ψ
Lower case:	δ	θ	ξ	ψ
Pronunciation:	TH	th	ks	ps

Now look at these words:

ψάρι	*psari*	fish
ταξί	*taksi*	taxi

The next five letters are:

Capital letter:	Φ	Λ	Π	Σ	Ω
Lower case:	φ	λ	π	σ, ς*	ω
Pronunciation :	*f*	*l*	*p*	*s*	*o*

*The form of this letter depends on its position in a word. **ς** is only used at the end of a word, otherwise **σ** is used, e.g. **σκύλος** (*skilos*) – dog.

The last letter is one to pay particular attention to as it not only looks unfamiliar but also represents an unfamiliar sound:

Γ γ (*gh* – see Pronunciation below)

For example:

γάτα	*ghata*	cat
μεγάλο	*meghalo*	big

Note also that a Greek question mark looks like an English semi-colon:

πόσο;	*poso?*	how much?

✔ Most Greek letters represent sounds similar to English

✔ There are four letters representing sounds which in English are made by putting two letters together:
Δ, δ (*TH*)   Θ, θ (*th*)   Ξ, ξ (*ks*)   Ψ, ψ (*ps*)

◎ Pronunciation tips

Greek is probably one of the easiest languages to read as what you see is generally what you hear. The Greek used today is very much simplified. The once prolific stress and breathing marks have been reduced to only one small mark above a vowel (e.g. ό) which indicates where the stress falls on a word (shown in the pronunciation by underlining).

The Greek vowels have simple pronunciations:

A, α	always pronounced "a" as in "bat"
E, ε	always pronounced "e" as in "bed"
I, ι/Y, υ/H, η	all pronounced "i" as in "tin"
O, o/Ω, ω	both pronounced "o" as in "pot"

A combination of two vowels may produce a different sound. Use the pronunciation guide for the individual words to help you. Note these especially:

αυ	pronounced "af" or "av", e.g. αυτοκίνητο (*aftokinito*) – "car"; αύριο (*avrio*) – "tomorrow"
ευ	pronounced "ef" or "ev", e.g. ευχαριστώ (*efharisto*) – "thank you"

Many of the other Greek letters are pronounced in a similar way to their English equivalents, but here are a few points to note:

P, ρ	pronounced trilled as the Scottish "r" at of the front of the mouth
X, χ	pronounced like the "ch" in the Yiddish "chutzpah"
Γ, γ	a combination of "w" as in "were" and "y" as in "yes"

◎ Summary of the Greek alphabet

The table below shows all the Greek letters, both capitals and lower case. You can refer to it as you work your way through the topics.

A	α	*a*	I	ι	*i*	P	ρ	*r*
B	β	*v*	K	κ	*k*	Σ	σ ς	*s*
Γ	γ	*gh*	Λ	λ	*l*	T	τ	*t*
Δ	δ	*TH* (as in "that")	M	μ	*m*	Y	υ	*i*
E	ε	*e*	N	ν	*n*	Φ	φ	*f*
Z	ζ	*z*	Ξ	ξ	*ks*	X	χ	*h*
H	η	*I*	O	o	*o*	Ψ	ψ	*ps*
Θ	θ	*th* (as in "thin")	Π	π	*p*	Ω	ω	*o*

8

① AROUND THE HOME

Look at the pictures of things you might find in a house.
Tear out the flashcards for this topic.
Follow steps 1 and 2 of the plan in the introduction.

παράθυρο
parathiro

καρέκλα
ka<u>re</u>kla

τραπέζι
trap<u>e</u>zi

τηλεόραση
tile<u>o</u>rasi

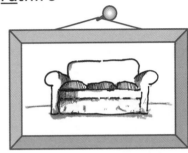

καναπές
kana<u>pes</u>

υπολογιστής
ipologhi<u>stis</u>

τηλέφωνο
til<u>e</u>fono

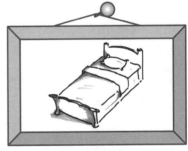

κρεβάτι
kre<u>v</u>ati

ψυγείο
psi<u>y</u>io

ντουλάπι
doo<u>la</u>pi

φούρνος
<u>foo</u>rnos

πόρτα
<u>po</u>rta

Match the pictures with the words, as in the example.

καναπές

κρεβάτι

παράθυρο

τραπέζι

τηλεόραση

υπολογιστής

τηλέφωνο

καρέκλα

Now match the Greek household words to the English.

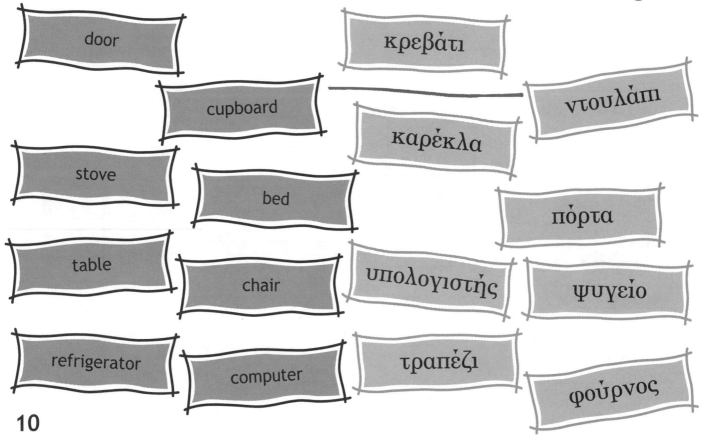

door

κρεβάτι

cupboard

ντουλάπι

καρέκλα

stove

bed

πόρτα

table

chair

υπολογιστής

ψυγείο

refrigerator

computer

τραπέζι

φούρνος

◎ **M**atch the words and their pronunciation.

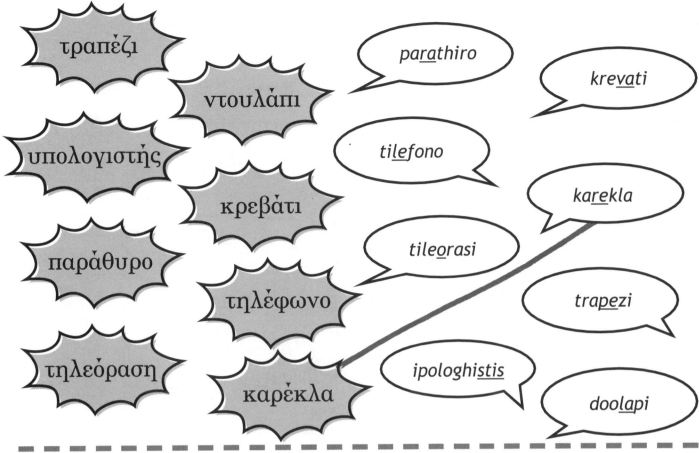

- -

◎ **S**ee if you can find these words in the word square.
The words can run left to right, or top to bottom:

φούρνος

κρεβάτι

καρέκλα

ψυγείο

πόρτα

καναπές

η	κ	α	ρ	έ	κ	λ	α
κ	τ	θ	μ	τ	π	σ	φ
ρ	κ	ψ	υ	γ	ε	ί	ο
ε	φ	π	ν	ρ	ν	α	ύ
β	ξ	ό	ν	ι	δ	γ	ρ
ά	κ	ρ	ε	β	ς	ψ	ν
τ	υ	τ	μ	φ	ω	ω	ο
ι	κ	α	ν	α	π	έ	ς

11

Decide where the household items should go. Then write the correct number in the picture, as in the example.

1. τραπέζι   2. καρέκλα   3. καναπές   4. τηλεόραση

5. τηλέφωνο   6. κρεβάτι   7. ντουλάπι   8. φούρνος

9. ψυγείο   10. υπολογιστής 11. παράθυρο 12. πόρτα

⊚ **N**ow see if you can fill in the household word at the bottom of the page by choosing the correct Greek.

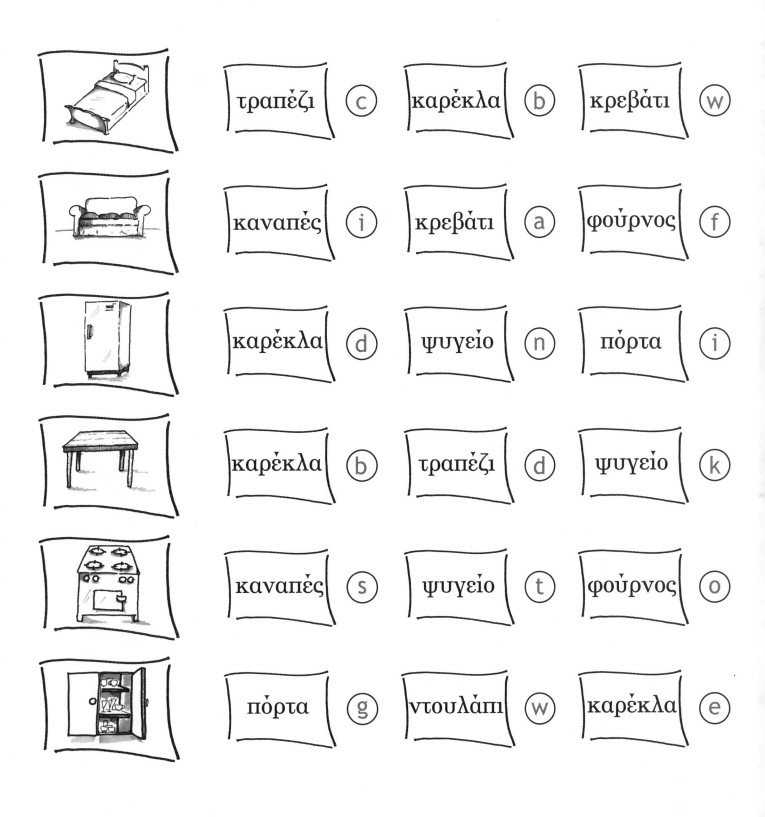

τραπἐζι ⓒ   καρἐκλα ⓑ   κρεβἀτι ⓦ

καναπἐς ⓘ   κρεβἀτι ⓐ   φοὐρνος ⓕ

καρἐκλα ⓓ   ψυγεἰο ⓝ   πὀρτα ⓘ

καρἐκλα ⓑ   τραπἐζι ⓓ   ψυγεἰο ⓚ

καναπἐς ⓢ   ψυγεἰο ⓣ   φοὐρνος ⓞ

πὀρτα ⓖ   ντουλἀπι ⓦ   καρἐκλα ⓔ

English word: ⓦ ◯ ◯ ◯ ◯ ◯

② CLOTHES

Look at the pictures of different clothes.
Tear out the flashcards for this topic.
Follow steps 1 and 2 of the plan in the introduction.

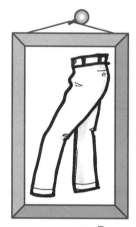

ζώνη
zoni

πουλόβερ
poolover

κάλτσα
kaltsa

αθλητικό
φανελλάκι
athlitiko fanelaki

σορτς
sorts

παντελόνι
pandeloni

φόρεμα
forema

καπέλο *kapelo*

επανωφόρι
epanofori

φούστα
foosta

παπούτσι
papootsi

πουκάμισο
pookamiso

14

◎ **M**atch the Greek words and their pronunciation.

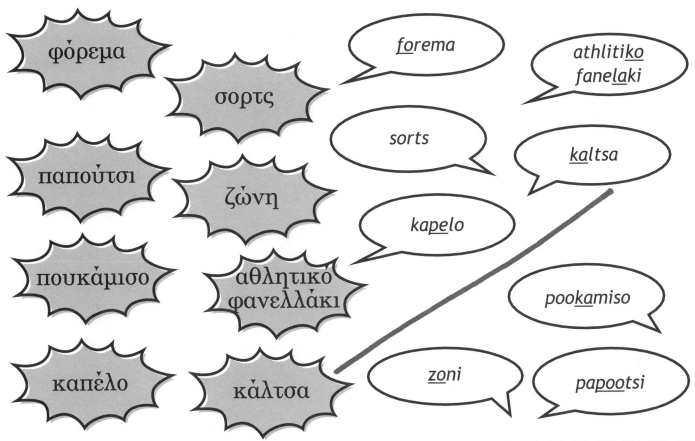

- -

◎ **S**ee if you can find these clothes in the word square.

The words can run left to right, or top to bottom:

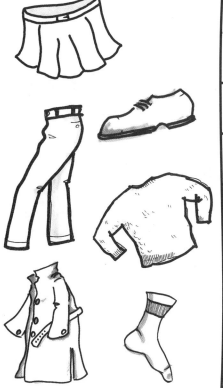

ε	π	α	ν	ω	φ	ό	ρ	ι
π	α	ν	τ	ε	λ	ό	ν	ι
ς	π	ύ	ω	λ	ύ	σ	τ	κ
π	ο	υ	λ	ό	β	ε	ρ	ά
ω	ύ	ν	δ	ψ	σ	υ	ω	λ
ι	τ	η	ρ	π	φ	α	β	τ
ε	σ	τ	ω	σ	δ	ς	ε	σ
λ	ι	κ	φ	ο	υ	σ	τ	α

15

Now match the Greek words, their pronunciation, and the English meaning, as in the example.

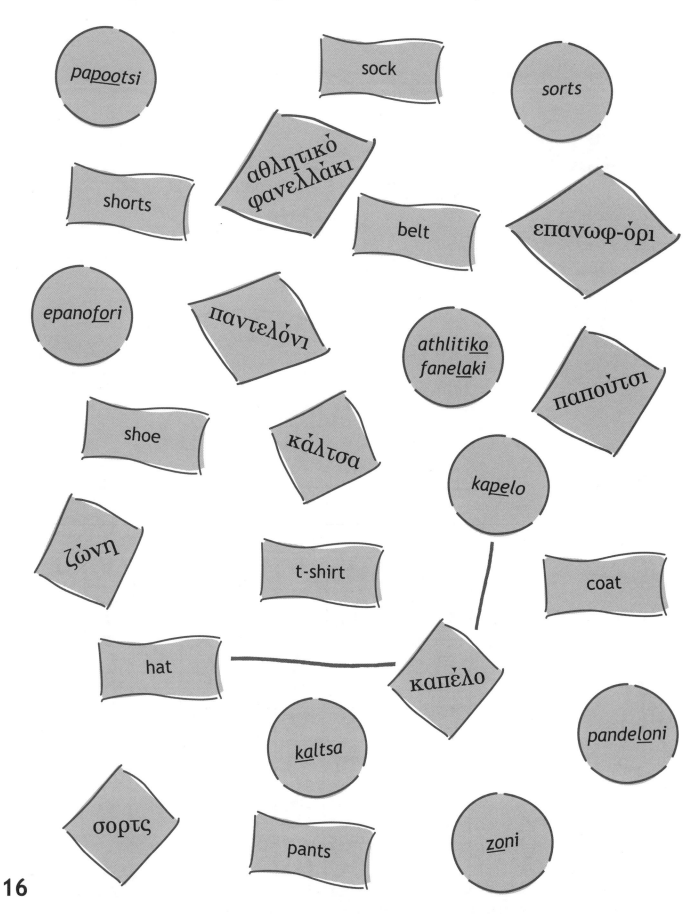

papootsi

sock

sorts

αθλητικό φανελλάκι

shorts

belt

επανωφ-όρι

epanofori

παντελόνι

athlitiko fanelaki

παπούτσι

shoe

κάλτσα

kapelo

ζώνη

t-shirt

coat

hat

καπέλο

pandeloni

kaltsa

σορτς

pants

zoni

Candy is going on vacation. Count how many of each type of clothing she is packing in her suitcase.

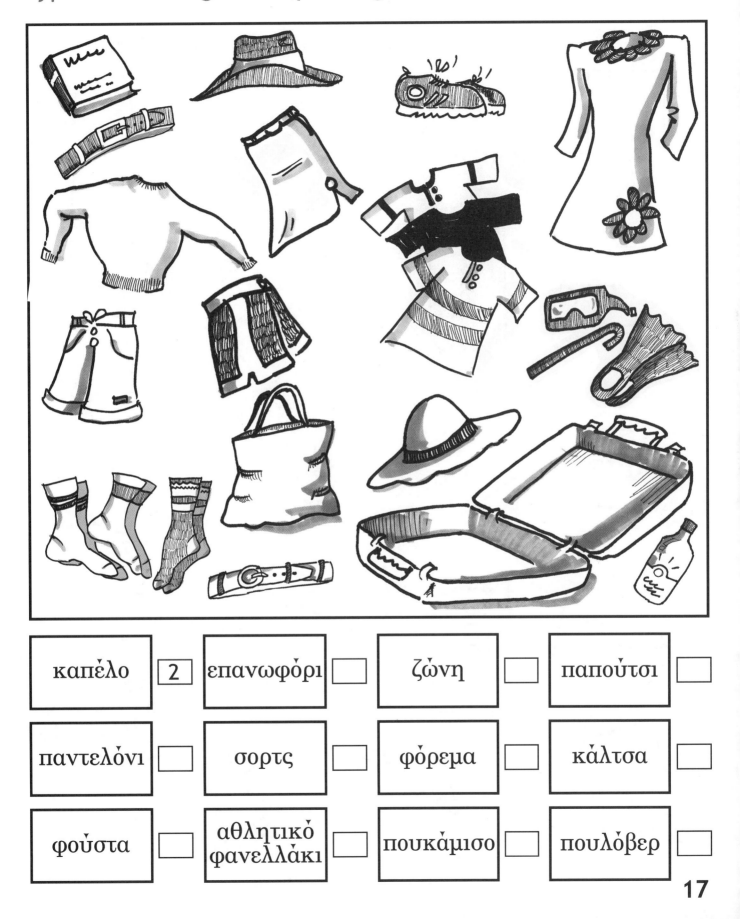

καπέλο	2	επανωφόρι		ζώνη		παπούτσι	
παντελόνι		σορτς		φόρεμα		κάλτσα	
φούστα		αθλητικό φανελλάκι		πουκάμισο		πουλόβερ	

Someone has ripped up the Greek words for clothes.
Can you join the two halves of the words, as in the example?

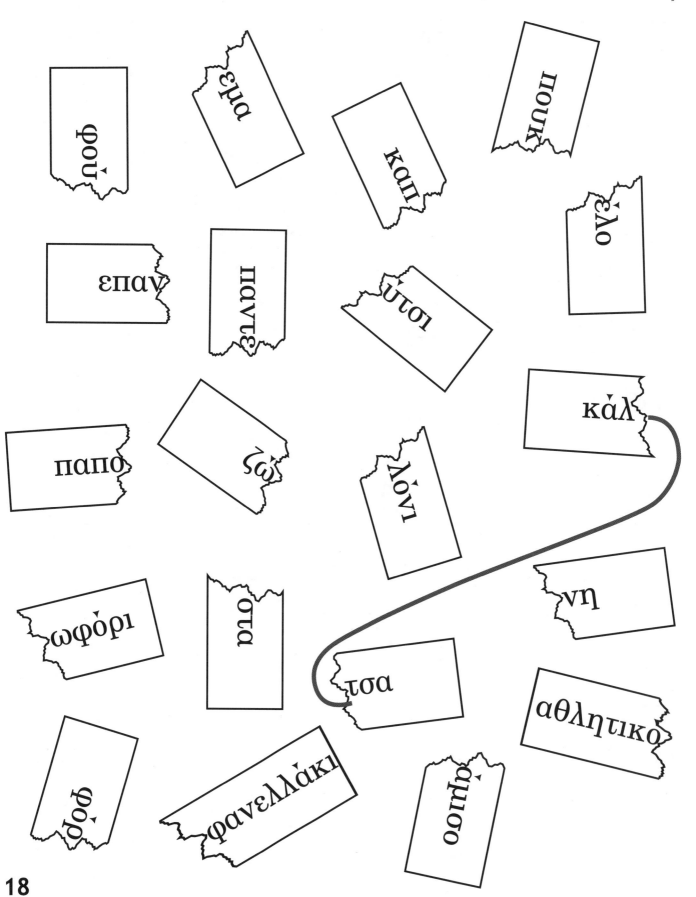

③ AROUND TOWN

Look at the pictures of things you might see around town.
Tear out the flashcards for this topic.
Follow steps 1 and 2 of the plan in the introduction.

ξενοδοχείο
ksenoᴛʜoʜio

λεωφορείο
*leofor_io_*

σπίτι   *sp_i_ti*

αυτοκίνητο
afto_ki_nito

κινηματογράφος
kinimato_g_rafos

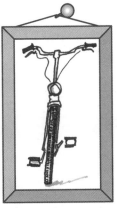

ποδήλατο
poᴛʜilato

τρένο
tr_e_no

ταξί   *ta_ksi_*

σχολείο   *shol_io_*

δρόμος   *ᴛʜromos*

κατάστημα
kat_a_stima

εστιατόριο
estia_to_rio

© **M**atch the Greek words to their English equivalents.

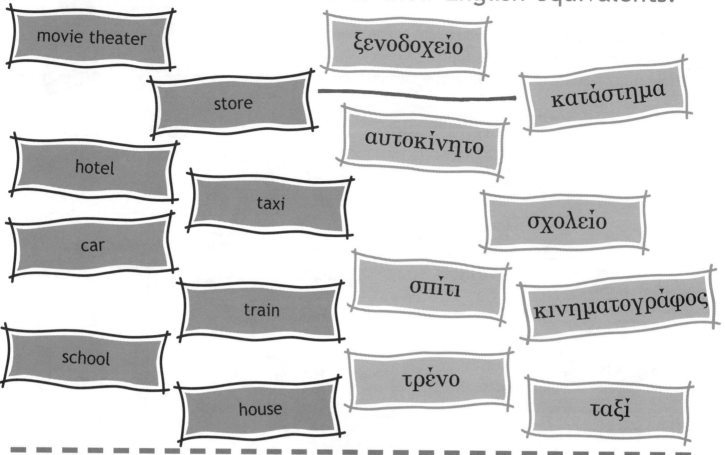

movie theater

ξενοδοχείο

κατάστημα

store

αυτοκίνητο

hotel

taxi

σχολείο

car

σπίτι

κινηματογράφος

train

school

τρένο

house

ταξί

© **N**ow put the English words in the same order as the Greek word chain, as in the example.

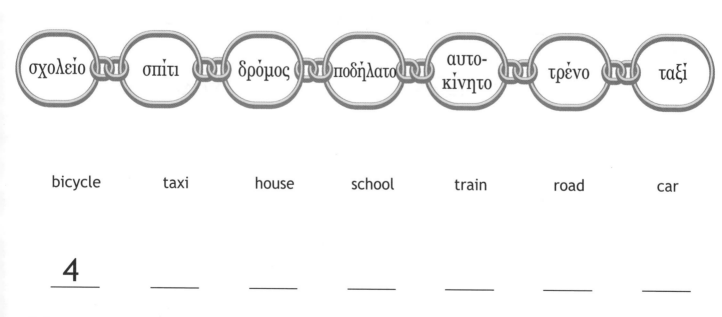

σχολείο | σπίτι | δρόμος | ποδήλατο | αυτο-κίνητο | τρένο | ταξί

bicycle   taxi   house   school   train   road   car

4 ___ ___ ___ ___ ___ ___ ___

20

⊚ **M**atch the words to the signs.

σχολείο   αυτοκίνητο   ποδήλατο   λεωφορείο

εστιατόριο   τρένο   ξενοδοχείο   ταξί

Now choose the Greek word that matches the picture to fill in the English word at the bottom of the page.

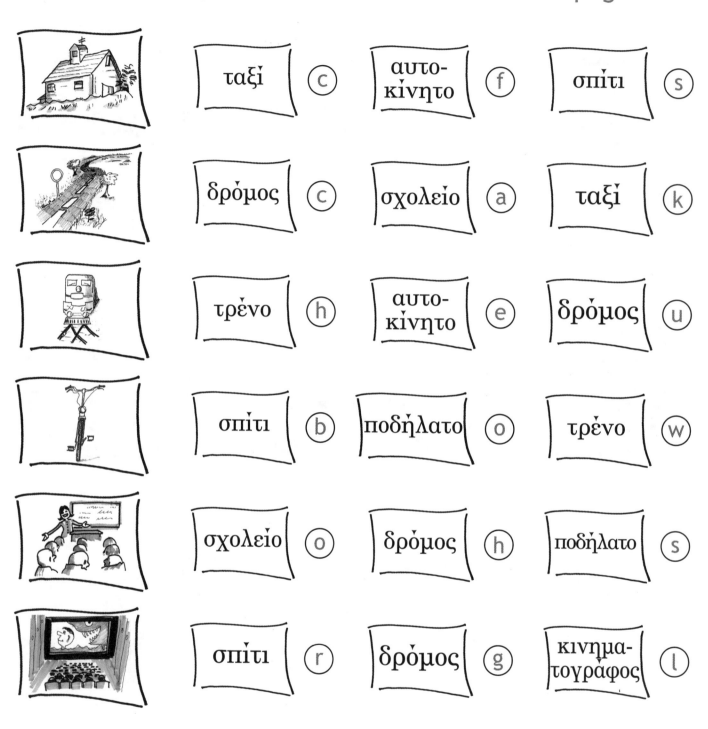

ταξί (c)	αυτο-κίνητο (f)	σπίτι (s)
δρόμος (c)	σχολείο (a)	ταξί (k)
τρένο (h)	αυτο-κίνητο (e)	δρόμος (u)
σπίτι (b)	ποδήλατο (o)	τρένο (w)
σχολείο (o)	δρόμος (h)	ποδήλατο (s)
σπίτι (r)	δρόμος (g)	κινημα-τογράφος (l)

English word: (s) ◯ ◯ ◯ ◯ ◯

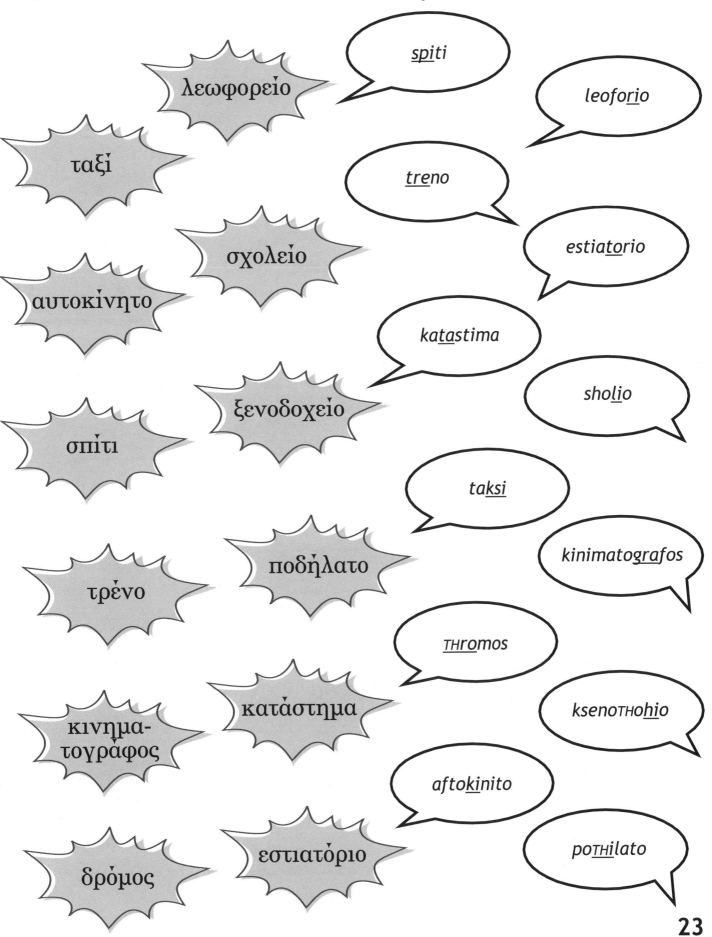

④ COUNTRYSIDE

Look at the pictures of things you might find in the countryside.
Tear out the flashcards for this topic.
Follow steps 1 and 2 of the plan in the introduction.

λόφος
lofos

γέφυρα
yefira

αγρόκτημα
aghroktima

βουνό
voono

λίμνη
limni

δέντρο
THendro

λουλούδι
looloοTHi

ποτάμι *potami*

θάλασσα
thalasa

χωράφι *horafi*

έρημος *erimos*

δάσος *THasos*

24

Can you match all the countryside words to the pictures.

βουνὸ

αγρόκτημα

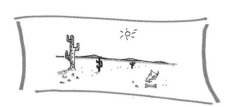 

θάλασσα

δάσος

ἔρημος

λόφος

λίμνη

γέφυρα

ποτάμι

λουλούδι

δέντρο

χωράφι

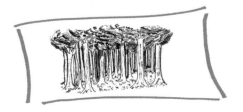 

25

Now check (✔) the features you can find in this landscape.

γέφυρα ✔   δέντρο ☐   έρημος ☐   λόφος ☐

βουνό ☐   θάλασσα ☐   χωράφι ☐   δάσος ☐

λίμνη ☐   ποτάμι ☐   λουλούδι ☐   αγρόκτημα ☐

Match the Greek words and their pronunciation.

βουνὸ

ποτὰμι

δὰσος

ἐρημος

θὰλασσα

αγρὸκτημα

γἐφυρα

χωρὰφι

erimos

aghroktima

horafi

THasos

potami

yefira

thalasa

voono

- - -

See if you can find these words in the word square.
The words can run left to right, or top to bottom.

δἐντρο

αγρὸκτημα

λὸφος

λουλοὺδι

γἐφυρα

λὶμνη

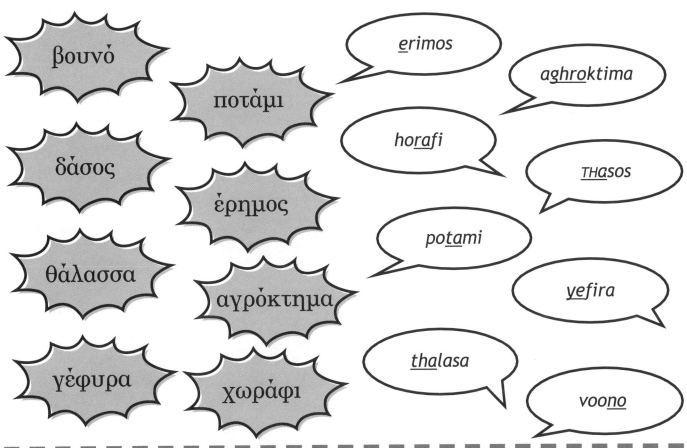

μ	ρ	ψ	λ	τ	υ	χ	κ	ι
γ	ο	ν	α	λ	ὸ	φ	ο	ς
ἐ	π	δ	η	υ	τ	ψ	ν	ρ
φ	ς	ἐ	λ	ι	μ	ν	η	γ
υ	φ	ν	κ	ς	ν	σ	τ	ς
ρ	λ	τ	μ	υ	φ	π	ψ	β
α	γ	ρ	ὸ	κ	τ	η	μ	α
δ	λ	ο	υ	λ	ο	ὺ	δ	ι

27

◎ **F**inally, test yourself by joining the Greek words, their pronunciation, and the English meanings, as in the example.

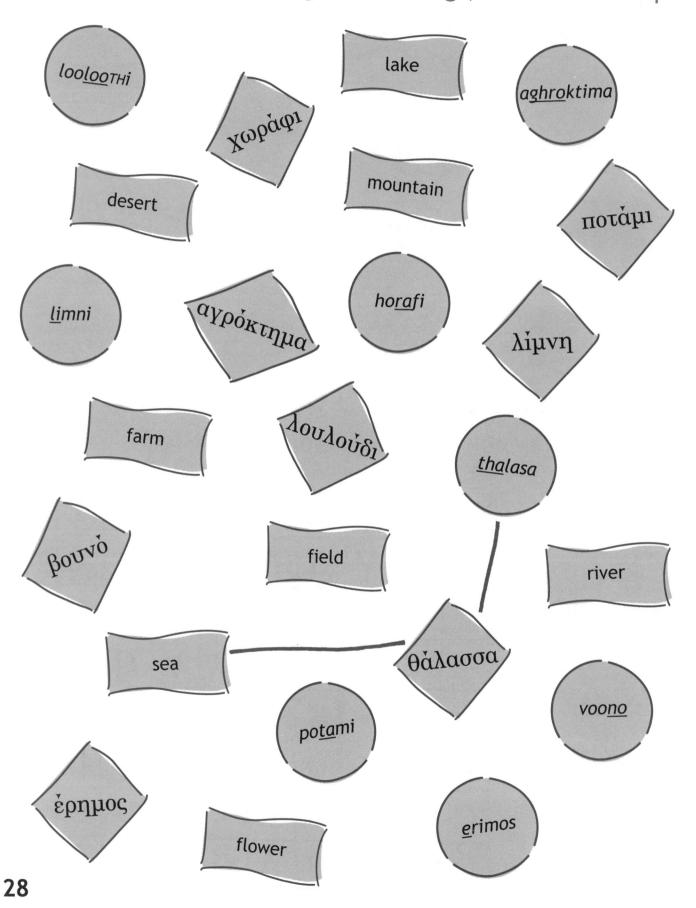

loolooTHi

lake

aghroktima

Χωράφι

desert

mountain

ποτάμι

limni

αγρόκτημα

horafi

λίμνη

farm

Λουλούδι

thalasa

βουνό

field

river

sea

θάλασσα

voono

potami

έρημος

erimos

flower

28

⑤ OPPOSITES

Look at the pictures.
Tear out the flashcards for this topic.
Follow steps 1 and 2 of the plan in the introduction.

βρώμικο
vromiko

καθαρό
katharo

μικρό
mikro

μεγάλο
meghalo

φθηνό *fthino*

ελαφρύ *elafri*

αργό *argho*

ακριβό *akrivo*

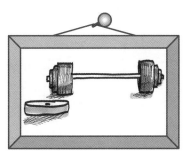

βαρύ *vari*

γρήγορο
ghrighoro

παλιό *palio*

καινούργιο
kenooryo

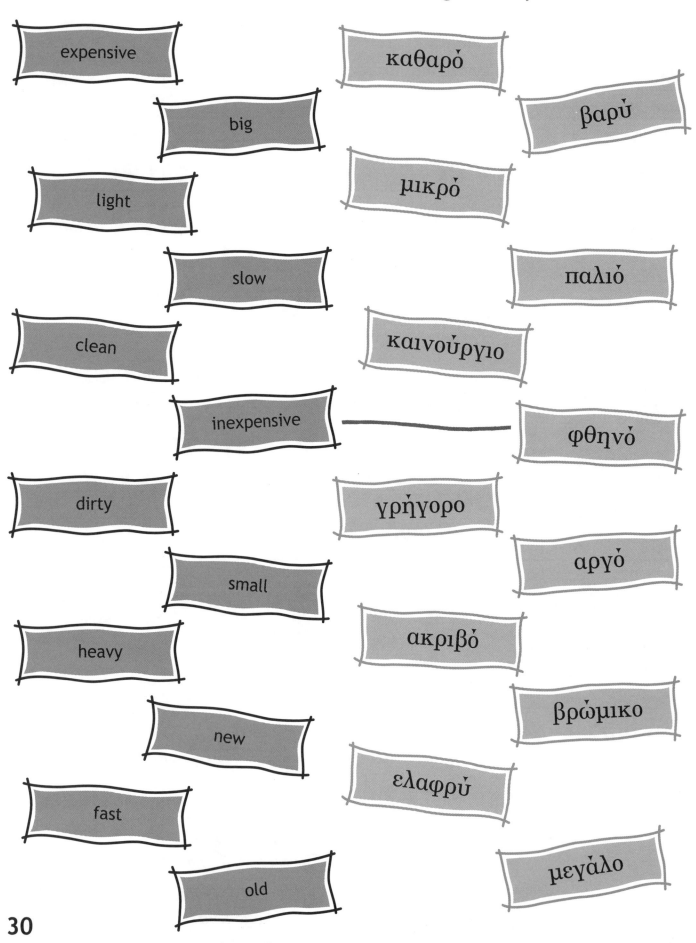

Join the Greek words to their English equivalents.

expensive

καθαρό

big

βαρύ

μικρό

light

slow

παλιό

clean

καινούργιο

inexpensive ———————— φθηνό

dirty

γρήγορο

αργό

small

ακριβό

heavy

βρώμικο

new

ελαφρύ

fast

old

μεγάλο

30

Now choose the Greek word that matches the picture
to fill in the English word at the bottom of the page.

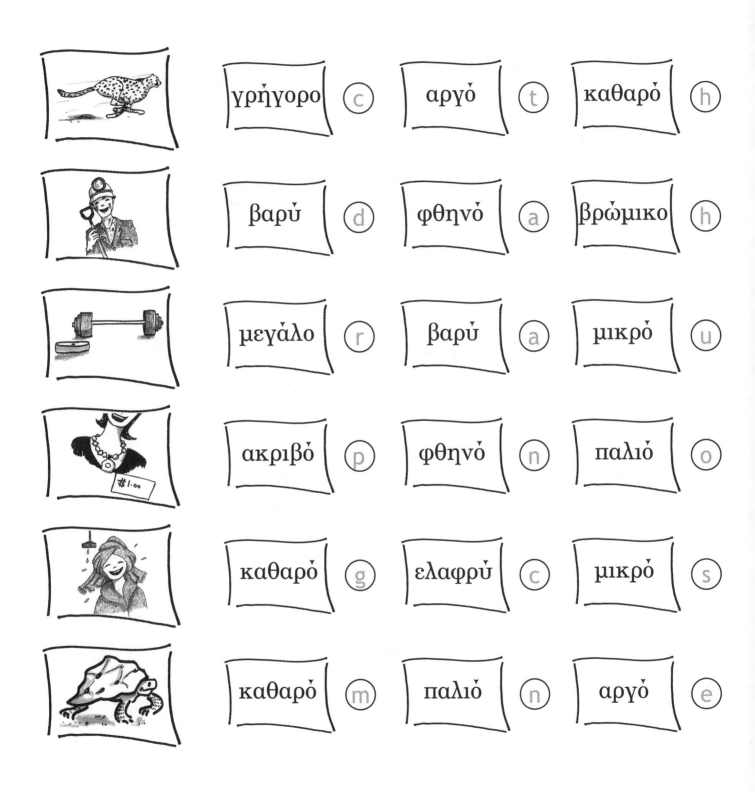

γρήγορο Ⓒ	αργό Ⓣ	καθαρό Ⓗ
βαρύ Ⓓ	φθηνό Ⓐ	βρώμικο Ⓗ
μεγάλο Ⓡ	βαρύ Ⓐ	μικρό Ⓤ
ακριβό Ⓟ	φθηνό Ⓝ	παλιό Ⓞ
καθαρό Ⓖ	ελαφρύ Ⓒ	μικρό Ⓢ
καθαρό Ⓜ	παλιό Ⓝ	αργό Ⓔ

English word: ◯ ◯ ◯ ◯ ◯ ◯

Find the odd one out in these groups of words.

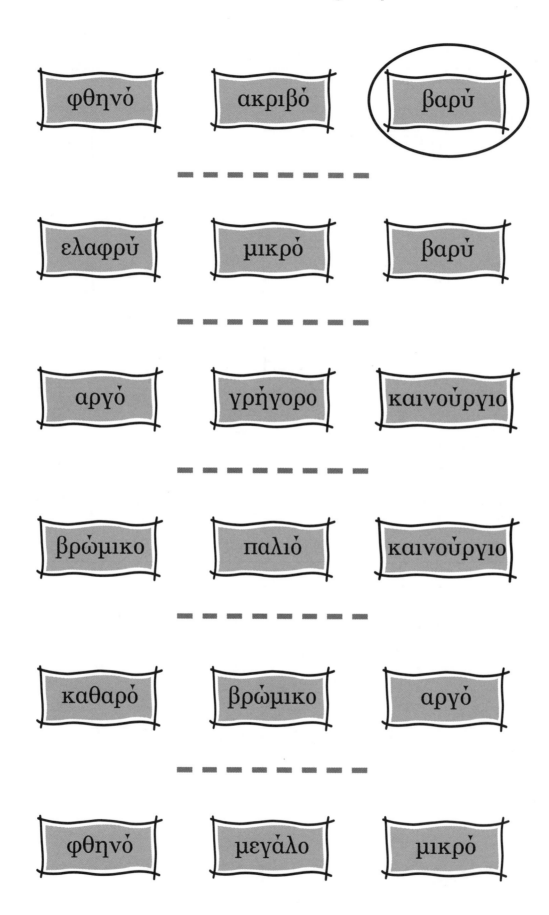

φθηνό	ακριβό	(βαρύ)
ελαφρύ	μικρό	βαρύ
αργό	γρήγορο	καινούργιο
βρώμικο	παλιό	καινούργιο
καθαρό	βρώμικο	αργό
φθηνό	μεγάλο	μικρό

◎ **F**inally, join the English words to their Greek opposites, as in the example.

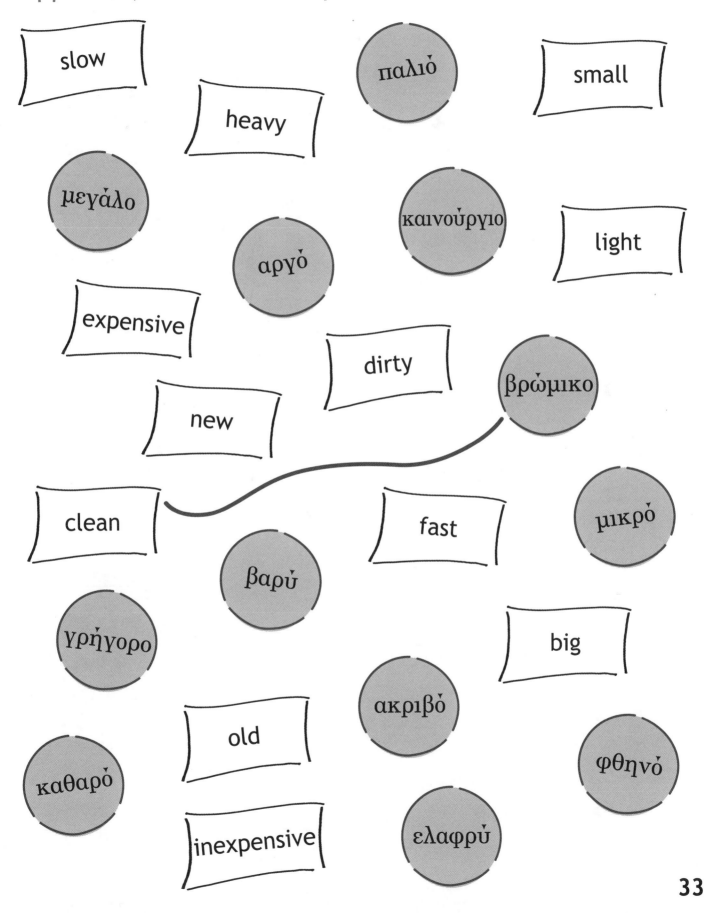

slow

παλιό

small

heavy

μεγάλο

καινούργιο

light

αργό

expensive

dirty

βρώμικο

new

clean

fast

μικρό

βαρύ

γρήγορο

big

ακριβό

old

φθηνό

καθαρό

inexpensive

ελαφρύ

⑥ ANIMALS

Look at the pictures.
Tear out the flashcards for this topic.
Follow steps 1 and 2 of the plan in the introduction.

πάπια *papia*

ελέφαντας
elefandas

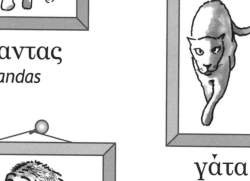

γάτα
ghata

σκύλος
skilos

κουνέλι
kooneli

μαϊμού
maimoo

ψάρι *psari*

πρόβατο *provato*

ποντίκι *pondiki*

αγελάδα
ayelaτηa

άλογο
alogho

λεοντάρι
leondari

34

Match the animals to their associated pictures, as in the example.

κουνέλι

άλογο

μαϊμού

γάτα

πρόβατο

ποντίκι

σκύλος

λεοντάρι

αγελάδα

ψάρι

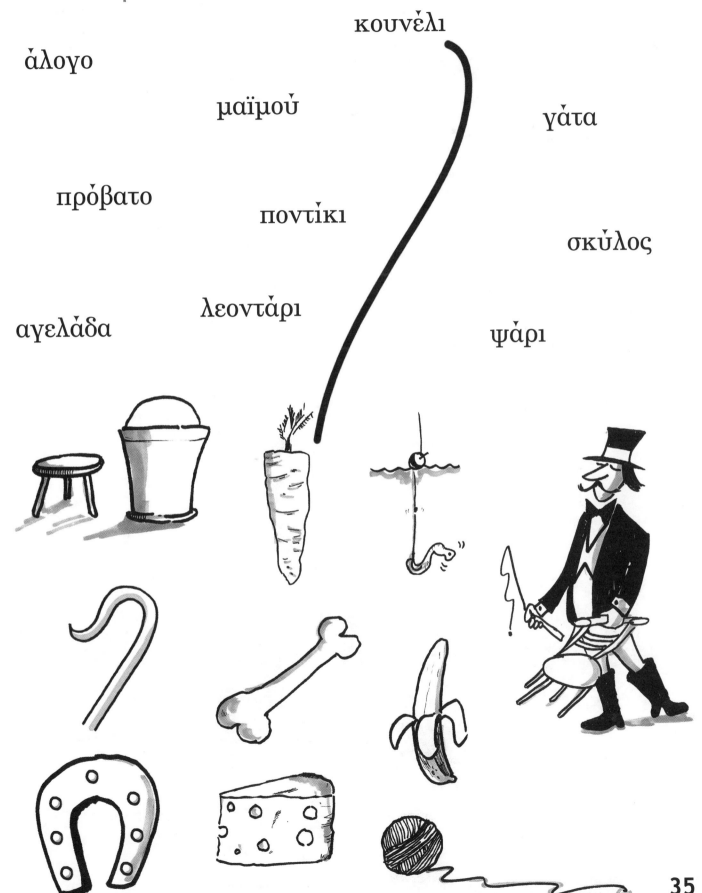

Now match the Greek to the pronunciation.

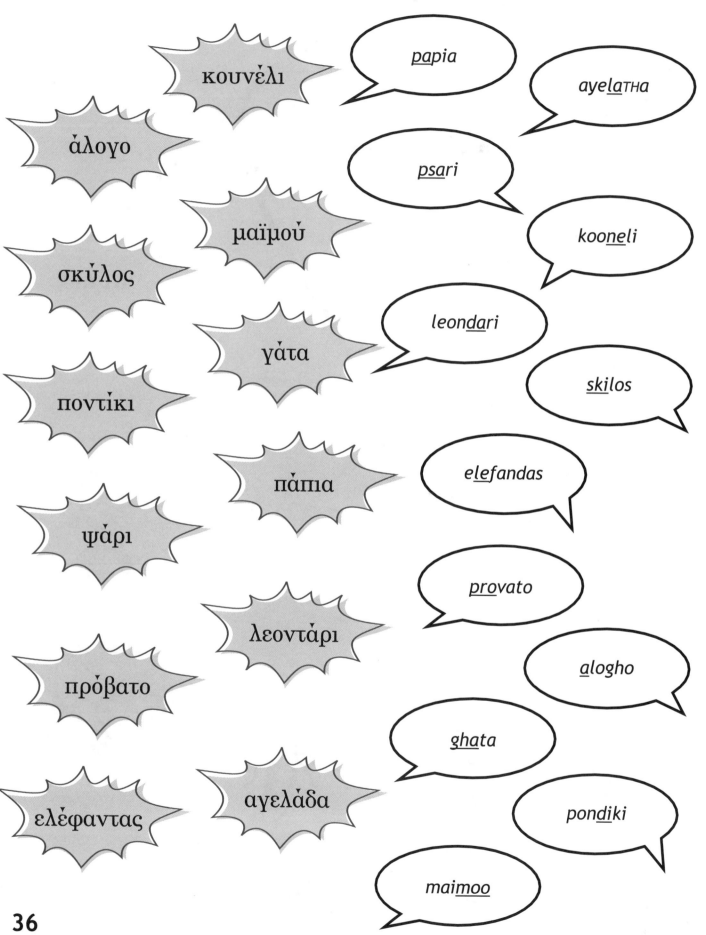

◎ **C**heck (✔) the animal words you can find in the word pile.

λίμνη

γάτα

σχολείο

αυτοκίνητο

κουνέλι

ελέφαντας

πρόβατο

κρεβάτι

βαρύ

παλιό

ταξί

παπούτσι

λόφος

λεοντάρι

αγελάδα

ψάρι

✔

☐

☐

☐

☐

☐

☐

☐

☐

☐

☐

☐

◎ Join the Greek animals to their English equivalents.

monkey

σκύλος

λεοντάρι

cow

mouse

μαϊμού

ελέφαντας

dog

sheep

κουνέλι

fish ——— ψάρι

lion

ποντίκι

πάπια

elephant

cat

αγελάδα

πρόβατο

duck

άλογο

rabbit

γάτα

horse

7 PARTS OF THE BODY

Look at the pictures of parts of the body.
Tear out the flashcards for this topic.
Follow steps 1 and 2 of the plan in the introduction.

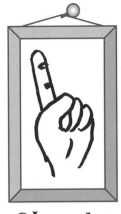

δάχτυλο
THahtilo

κεφάλι
kefali

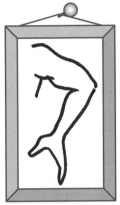

βραχίονας
vrahionas

μάτι _mati_

πλάτη
plati

χέρι
heri

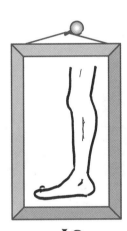

πόδι
poTHi

μαλλιά _malia_

στομάχι
stomahi

αυτί _afti_

μύτη _miti_

στόμα _stoma_

39

⊚ **S**omeone has ripped up the Greek words for parts of the body. Can you join the two halves of the word again?

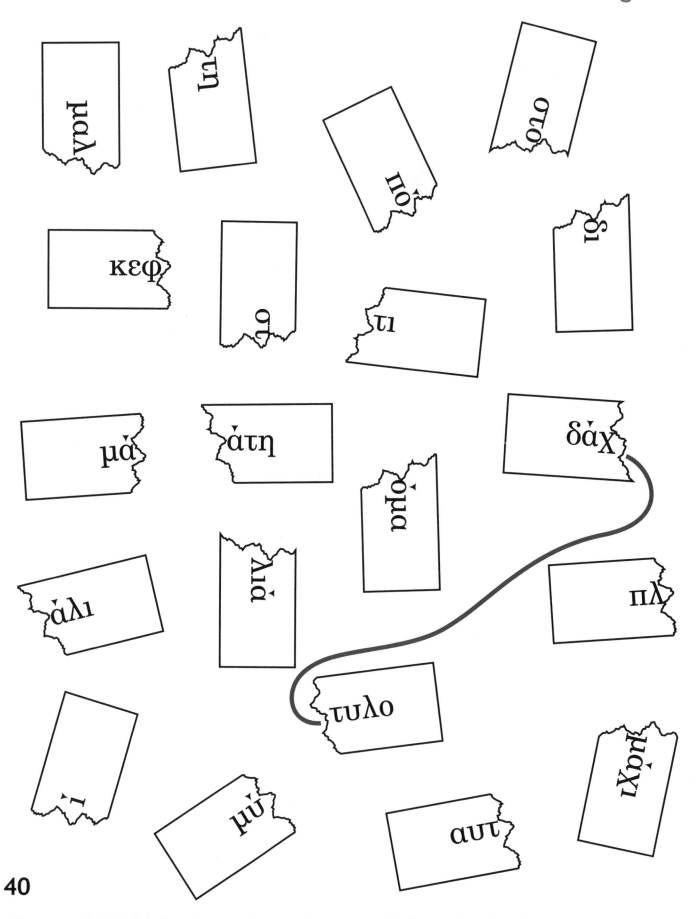

◎ **S**ee if you can find and circle six parts of the body in the word square, then draw them in the boxes below.

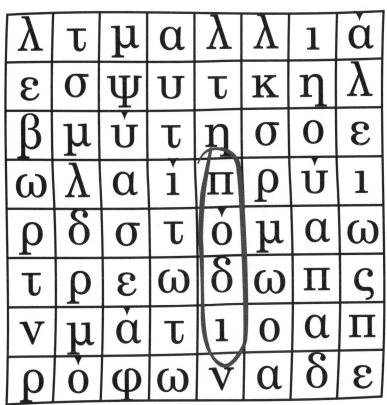

The words can run left to right, or top to bottom:

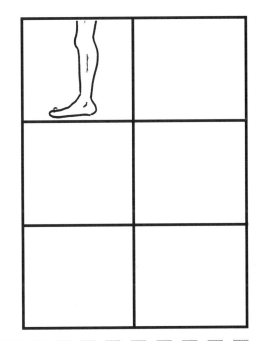

- -

◎ **N**ow match the Greek to the pronunciation.

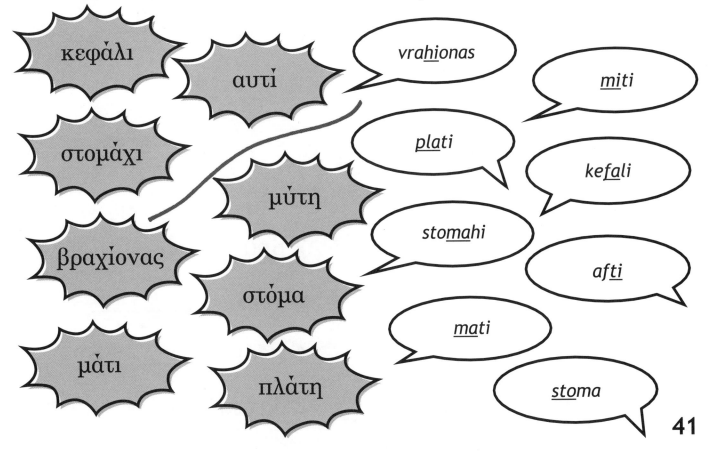

◎ **L**abel the body with the correct number, and write the pronunciation next to the words.

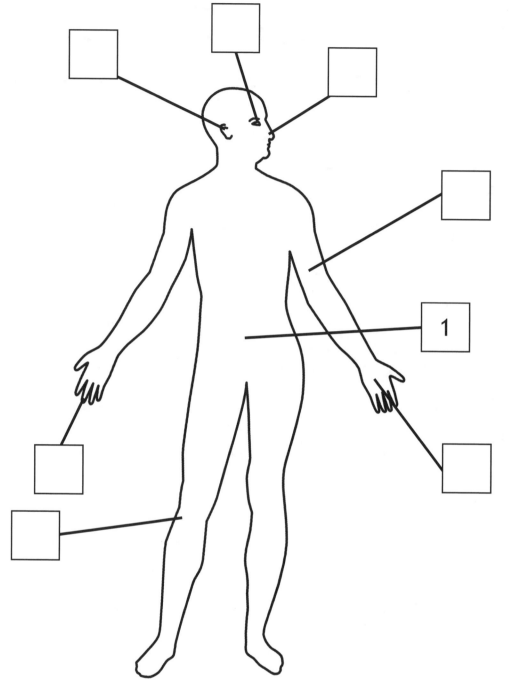

1 στομάχι *stomahi*

2 βραχίονας _____

3 μύτη _____

4 χέρι _____

5 αυτί _____

6 πόδι _____

7 μάτι _____

8 δάχτυλο _____

◎ **F**inally, match the Greek words, their pronunciation, and the English meanings, as in the example.

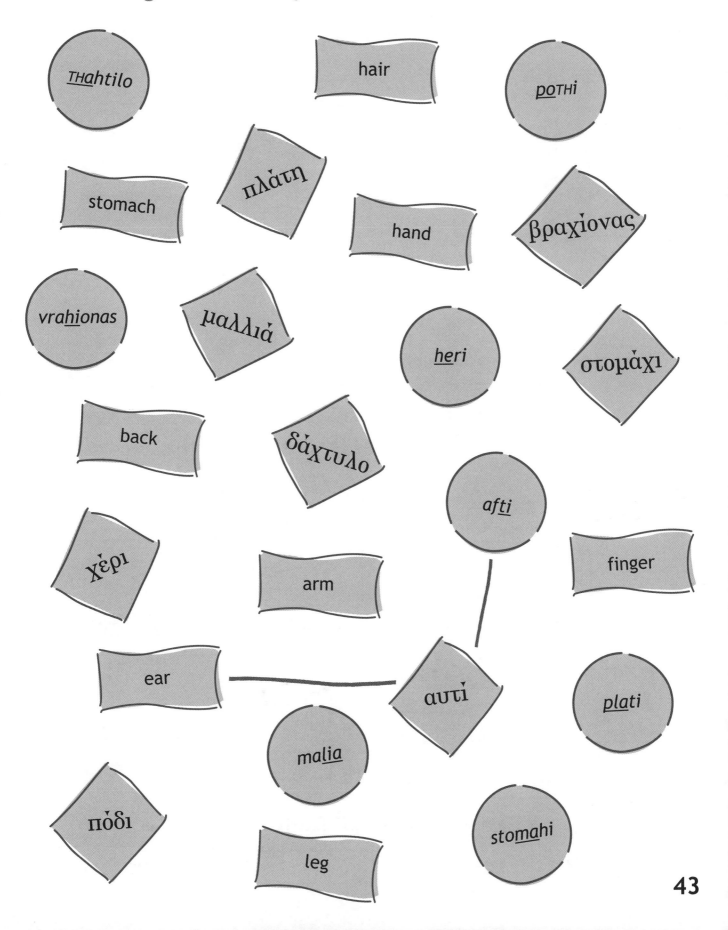

тнаhtilo

hair

ротнi

стomach

πλάτη

hand

βραχίονας

vrahionas

μαλλιά

heri

στομάχι

back

δάχτυλο

afti

χέρι

arm

finger

ear

αυτί

plati

malia

πόδι

stomahi

leg

43

⑧ USEFUL EXPRESSIONS

Look at the pictures.
Tear out the flashcards for this topic.
Follow steps 1 and 2 of the plan in the introduction.

πού; *poo?*

όχι *ohi*

ναι *ne*

γειά *ya*

αντίο *andio*

χθες *hthes*

σήμερα *simera*

αύριο *avrio*

εδώ *eTHO*

εκεί *eki*

τώρα *tora*

πόσο; *poso?*

συγγνώμη *sighnomi*

υπέροχα! *iperoha!*

παρακαλώ *parakalo*

ευχαριστώ *efharisto*

44

◎ **M**atch the Greek words to their English equivalents.

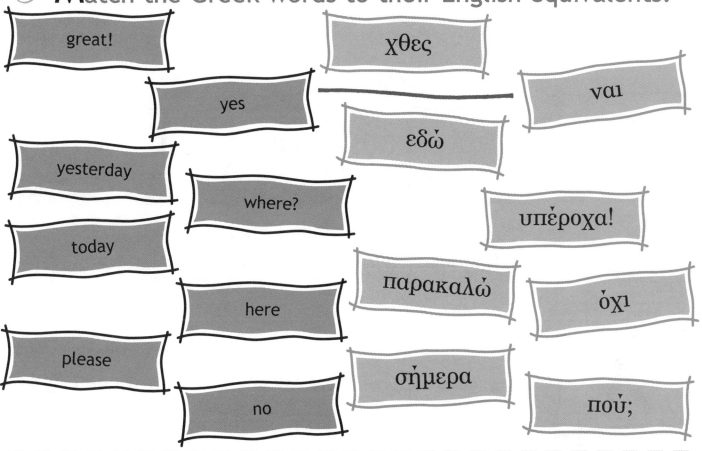

great!

yes

χθες

ναι

εδώ

yesterday

where?

υπέροχα!

today

παρακαλώ

όχι

here

please

σήμερα

no

πού;

◎ **N**ow match the Greek to the pronunciation.

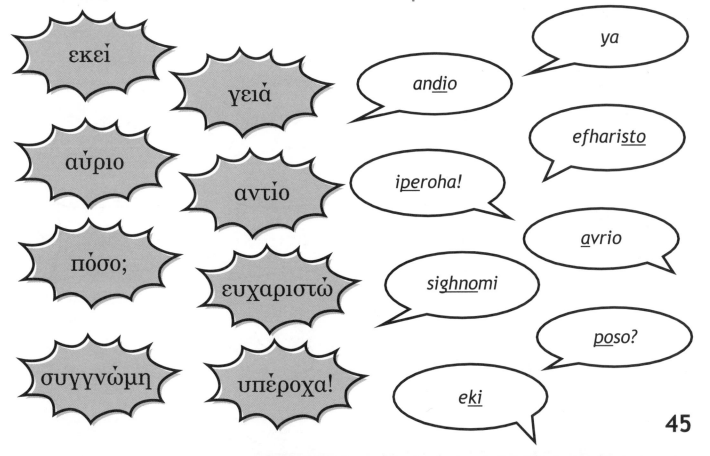

εκεί

γειά

ya

andio

αύριο

efharisto

αντίο

iperoha!

πόσο;

avrio

ευχαριστώ

sighnomi

poso?

συγγνώμη

υπέροχα!

eki

45

Choose the Greek word that matches the picture to fill in the English word at the bottom of the page.

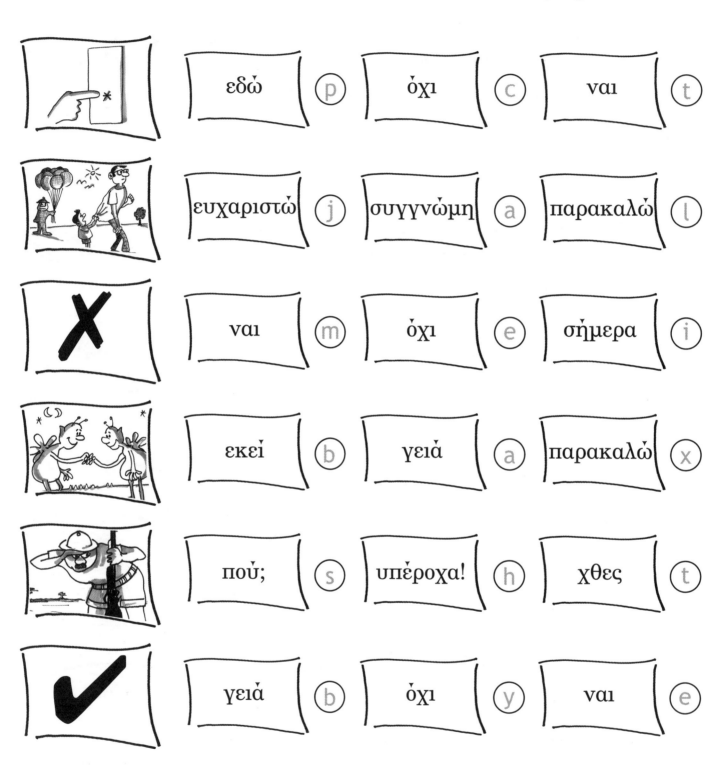

εδώ (p)	όχι (c)	ναι (t)
ευχαριστώ (j)	συγγνώμη (a)	παρακαλώ (l)
ναι (m)	όχι (e)	σήμερα (i)
εκεί (b)	γειά (a)	παρακαλώ (x)
πού; (s)	υπέροχα! (h)	χθες (t)
γειά (b)	όχι (y)	ναι (e)

English word: (p) ○ ○ ○ ○ ○

46

What are these people saying? Write the correct number in each speech bubble, as in the example.

1. γειά   2. παρακαλώ   3. ναι   4. όχι

5. εδώ   6. συγγνώμη   7. πού;   8. πόσο;

◎ **F**inally, match the Greek words, their pronunciation, and the English meanings, as in the example.

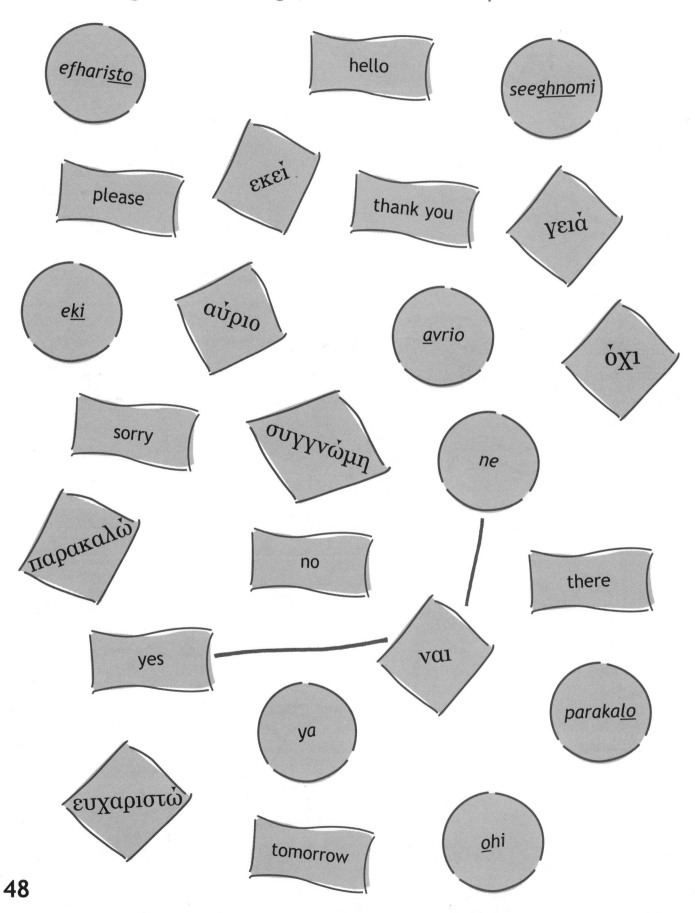

efharisto

hello

seeghnomi

please

εκεὶ

thank you

γειά

eki

αὐριο

avrio

ὀχι

sorry

συγγνὼμη

ne

παρακαλὼ

no

there

yes

ναι

ya

parakalo

ευχαριστὼ

tomorrow

ohi

● ROUND-UP

This section is designed to review all the 100 words you have met in the different topics. It is a good idea to test yourself with your flashcards before trying this section.

- -

◎ These ten objects are hidden in the picture. Can you find and circle them?

πόρτα	λουλούδι	κρεβάτι	επανωφόρι	καπέλο
ποδήλατο	καρέκλα	σκύλος	ψάρι	κάλτσα

© See if you can remember all these words.

σήμερα

λεωφορείο

γρήγορο

μύτη

έρημος

ναι

ντουλάπι

λεοντάρι

φόρεμα

φθηνό

ποτάμι

πόδι

50

Find the odd one out in these groups of words and say why.

| σκύλος | αγελάδα | **(τραπέζι)** | μαϊμού |

Because it isn't an animal.

- - - - - - - - - -

| αυτοκίνητο | λεωφορείο | τρένο | τηλέφωνο |

- - - - - - - - - -

| αυτοκίνητο | επανωφόρι | πουκάμισο | φούστα |

- - - - - - - - - -

| θάλασσα | λίμνη | ποτάμι | δέντρο |

- - - - - - - - - -

| ακριβό | βρώμικο | καθαρό | κινημα-τογράφος |

- - - - - - - - - -

| κουνέλι | γάτα | ψάρι | λεοντάρι |

- - - - - - - - - -

| βραχίονας | καναπές | κεφάλι | στομάχι |

- - - - - - - - - -

| παρακαλώ | χθες | αύριο | σήμερα |

- - - - - - - - - -

| φούρνος | κρεβάτι | ντουλάπι | ψυγείο |

Look at the objects below for 30 seconds.

Cover the picture and try to remember all the objects.
Circle the Greek words for those you remember.

λουλούδι   παπούτσι   ευχαριστώ   πόρτα

αυτοκίνητο   εδώ   επανωφόρι   τρένο
όχι

ζώνη   βουνό   καρέκλα   άλογο

κάλτσα   μάτι   κρεβάτι

αθλητικό
φανελλάκι
σορτς   ταξί   τηλεόραση   μαϊμού

Now match the Greek words, their pronunciation, and the English meanings, as in the example.

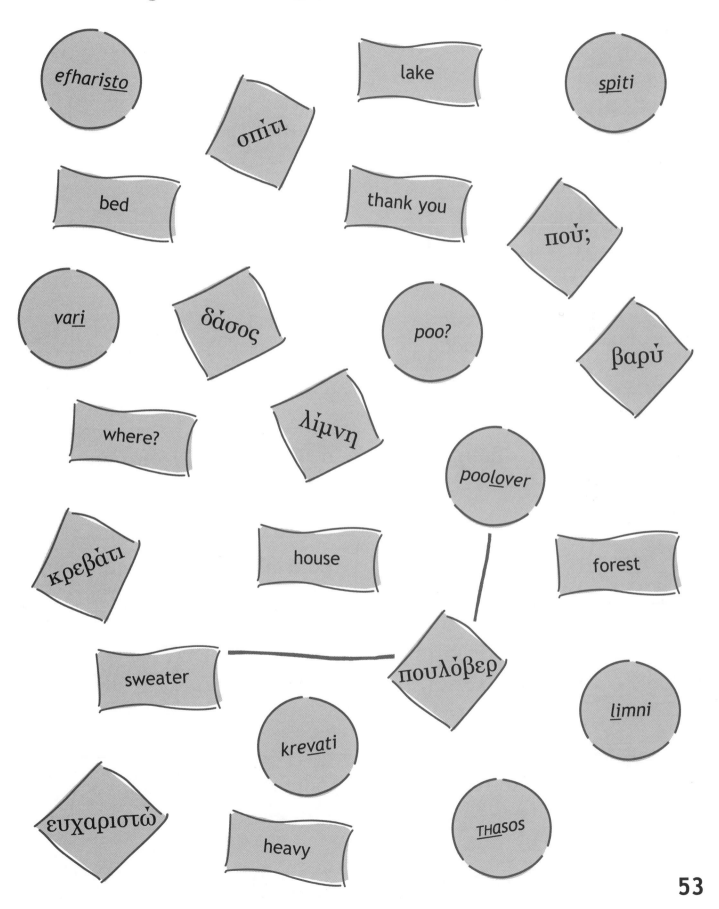

efharisto

lake

spiti

σπίτι

bed

thank you

πού;

vari

δάσος

poo?

βαρύ

where?

λίμνη

poolover

κρεβάτι

house

forest

sweater

πουλόβερ

limni

krevati

ευχαριστώ

heavy

тнasos

⊚ **F**ill in the English phrase at the bottom of the page.

καναπές (w)	ταξί (g)	αυτί (t)
πάπια (o)	βρώμικο (a)	γέφυρα (e)
ναι (m)	πόσο; (l)	σήμερα (i)
αγελάδα (b)	παράθυρο (l)	κάλτσα (h)
πού; (e)	στόμα (a)	σκύλος (d)
μάτι (o)	τραπέζι (p)	γειά (v)
λόφος (n)	όχι (y)	ποτάμι (r)
κουνέλι (n)	δρόμος (e)	φούρνος (s)

54   **E**nglish phrase: (w) ( ) ( ) ( )   ( ) ( ) ( ) ( ) !

Look at the two pictures and check (✔) the objects that are different in Picture B.

σορτς	☐
αθλητικό φανελλάκι	☐
πόρτα	☐
γάτα	☐
καρέκλα	☐
ψάρι	☐
κάλτσα	☐
σκύλος	☐

Picture A

Picture B

Now join the Greek words to their English equivalents.

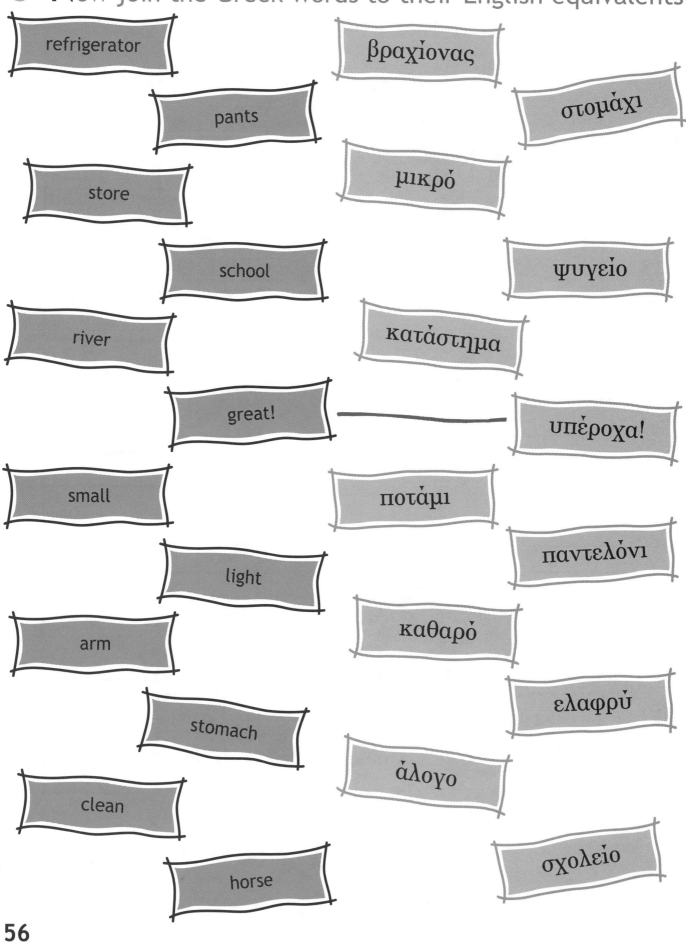

refrigerator

βραχὶονας

στομὰχι

pants

μικρὸ

store

school

ψυγεὶο

river

κατὰστημα

great! — υπὲροχα!

small

ποτὰμι

παντελὸνι

light

καθαρὸ

arm

ελαφρὺ

stomach

ὰλογο

clean

σχολεὶο

horse

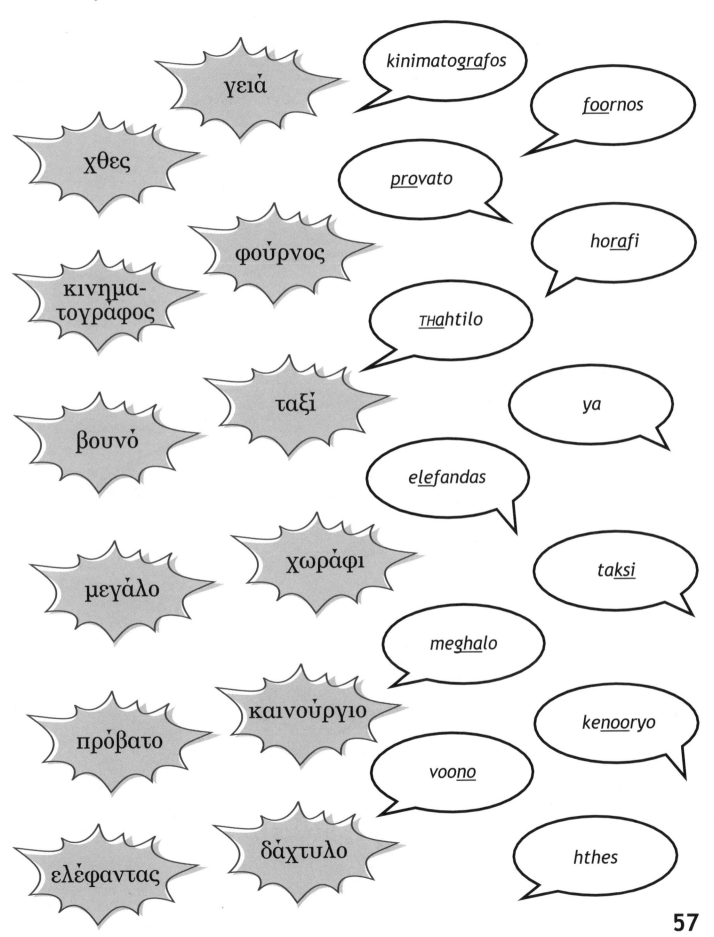

Snake game.

- You will need a die and counter(s). You can challenge yourself to reach the finish or play with someone else. You have to throw the exact number to finish.

- Throw the die and move forward that number of spaces. When you land on a word you must pronounce it and say what it means in English. If you can't, you have to go back to the square you came from.

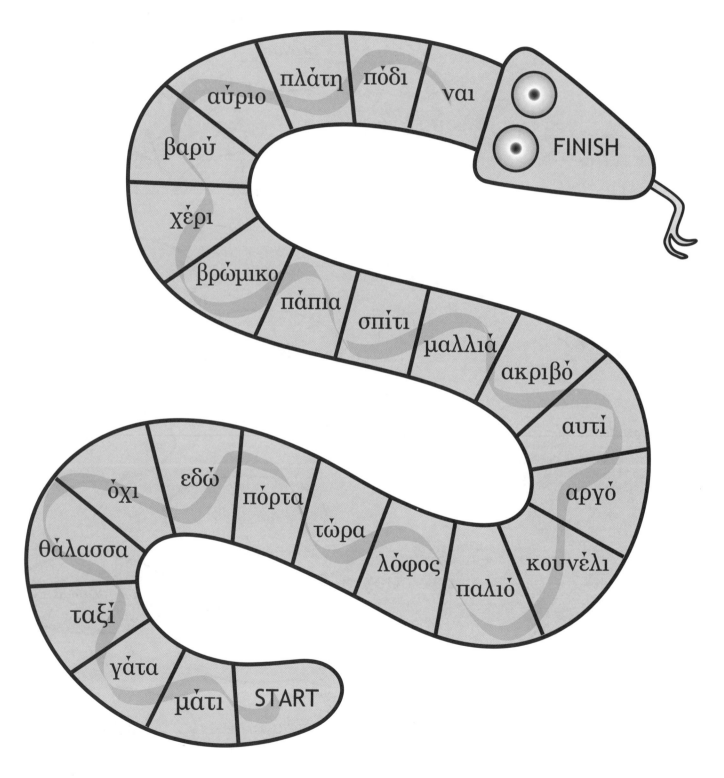

⊚ Answers

❶ Around the home

Page 10 (top)
See page 9 for correct picture.

Page 10 (bottom)
door	πόρτα
cupboard	ντουλάπι
stove	φούρνος
bed	κρεβάτι
table	τραπέζι
chair	καρέκλα
refrigerator	ψυγείο
computer	υπολογιστής

Page 11 (top)
τραπέζι	trapezi
ντουλάπι	doolapi
υπολογιστής	ipologhistis
κρεβάτι	krevati
παράθυρο	parathiro
τηλέφωνο	tilefono
τηλεόραση	tileorasi
καρέκλα	karekla

Page 11 (bottom)

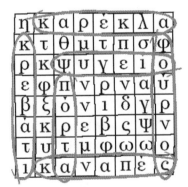

Page 12

Page 13
English word: window

❷ Clothes

Page 15 (top)
φόρεμα	forema
σορτς	sorts
παπούτσι	papootsi
ζώνη	zoni
πουκάμισο	pookamiso
αθλητικό φανελλάκι	athlitiko fanelaki
καπέλο	kapelo
κάλτσα	kaltsa

Page 15 (bottom)

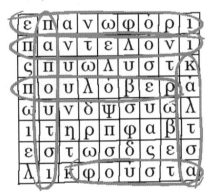

Page 16
hat	καπέλο	kapelo
shoe	παπούτσι	papootsi
sock	κάλτσα	kaltsa
shorts	σορτς	sorts
t-shirt	αθλητικό φανελλάκι	athlitiko fanelaki
belt	ζώνη	zoni
coat	επανωφόρι	epanofori
pants	παντελόνι	pandeloni

Page 17
καπέλο (hat)	2
επανωφόρι (coat)	0
ζώνη (belt)	2
παπούτσι (shoe)	2 (1 pair)
παντελόνι (pants)	0
σορτς (shorts)	2
φόρεμα (dress)	1
κάλτσα (sock)	6 (3 pairs)
φούστα (skirt)	1
αθλητικό φανελλάκι (t-shirt)	3
πουκάμισο (shirt)	0
πουλόβερ (sweater)	1

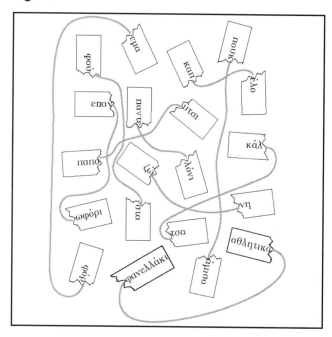

❸ AROUND TOWN

Page 20 (top)

movie theater	κινηματογράφος
store	κατάστημα
hotel	ξενοδοχείο
taxi	ταξί
car	αυτοκίνητο
train	τρένο
school	σχολείο
house	σπίτι

Page 20 (bottom)

bicycle	4
taxi	7
house	2
school	1
train	6
road	3
car	5

Page 21

σχολείο   ταξί   λεωφορείο

αυτοκίνητο   τρένο   εστιατόριο

ξενοδοχείο   ποδήλατο

60

Page 22

English word: school

Page 23

λεωφορείο	leofo<u>ri</u>o
ταξί	<u>taksi</u>
σχολείο	sho<u>li</u>o
αυτοκίνητο	afto<u>ki</u>nito
ξενοδοχείο	ksenoτHo<u>hi</u>o
σπίτι	<u>spiti</u>
ποδήλατο	poτH<u>i</u>lato
τρένο	<u>treno</u>
κατάστημα	kat<u>a</u>stima
κινηματογράφος	kinimato<u>grafos</u>
εστιατόριο	estia<u>to</u>rio
δρόμος	<u>THro</u>mos

❹ COUNTRYSIDE

Page 25

See page 24 for correct picture.

Page 26

γέφυρα	✔	χωράφι	✔
δέντρο	✔	δάσος	✔
έρημος	✘	λίμνη	✘
λόφος	✘	ποτάμι	✔
βουνό	✔	λουλούδι	✔
θάλασσα	✘	αγρόκτημα	✔

Page 27 (top)

βουνό	voo<u>no</u>
ποτάμι	po<u>ta</u>mi
δάσος	<u>THa</u>sos
έρημος	<u>e</u>rimos
θάλασσα	<u>tha</u>lasa
αγρόκτημα	a<u>ghro</u>ktima
γέφυρα	<u>ye</u>fira
χωράφι	ho<u>ra</u>fi

Page 27 (bottom)

μ	ρ	ψ	λ	τ	υ	χ	κ	ι
γ	ο	ν	α	λ	ό	φ	ο	ς
ε	π	δ	η	υ	τ	ψ	ν	ρ
φ	ς	ε	λ	ί	μ	ν	η	γ
υ	φ	ν	κ	ς	ν	σ	τ	ς
ρ	λ	τ	μ	υ	φ	π	ψ	β
α	γ	ρ	ό	κ	τ	ω	μ	α
δ	λ	ο	υ	λ	ο	υ	δ	ι

Page 28

sea	θάλασσα	*thalasa*
lake	λίμνη	*limni*
desert	έρημος	*erimos*
farm	αγρόκτημα	*aghroktima*
flower	λουλούδι	*looloothi*
mountain	βουνό	*voono*
river	ποτάμι	*potami*
field	χωράφι	*horafi*

❺ OPPOSITES

Page 30

expensive	ακριβό
big	μεγάλο
light	ελαφρύ
slow	αργό
clean	καθαρό
inexpensive	φθηνό
dirty	βρώμικο
small	μικρό
heavy	βαρύ
new	καινούργιο
fast	γρήγορο
old	παλιό

Page 31

English word: change

Page 32

Odd one outs are those which are not opposites:

βαρύ
μικρό
καινούργιο
βρώμικο
αργό
φθηνό

Page 33

old	καινούργιο
big	μικρό
new	παλιό
slow	γρήγορο
dirty	καθαρό
small	μεγάλο
heavy	ελαφρύ
clean	βρώμικο
light	βαρύ
expensive	φθηνό
inexpensive	ακριβό

❻ ANIMALS

Page 35

 αγελάδα   κουνέλι   ψάρι   λεοντάρι

πρόβατο   σκύλος   μαϊμού

 άλογο   ποντίκι   γάτα

Page 36

κουνέλι	*kooneli*
άλογο	*alogho*
μαϊμού	*maimoo*
σκύλος	*skilos*
γάτα	*ghata*
ποντίκι	*pondiki*
πάπια	*papia*
ψάρι	*psari*
λεοντάρι	*leondari*
πρόβατο	*provato*
αγελάδα	*ayelatha*
ελέφαντας	*elefandas*

Page 37

elephant	✔	mouse	✘
monkey	✘	cat	✔
sheep	✔	dog	✘
lion	✔	cow	✔
fish	✔	horse	✘
duck	✘	rabbit	✔

Page 38

monkey	μαϊμού
cow	αγελάδα
mouse	ποντίκι
dog	σκύλος
sheep	πρόβατο
fish	ψάρι
lion	λεοντάρι
elephant	ελέφαντας
cat	γάτα
duck	πάπια
rabbit	κουνέλι
horse	άλογο

❼ PARTS OF THE BODY

Page 40

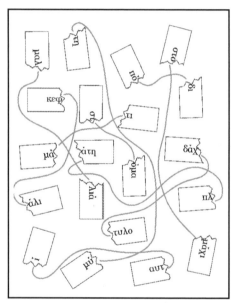

Page 41 (top)

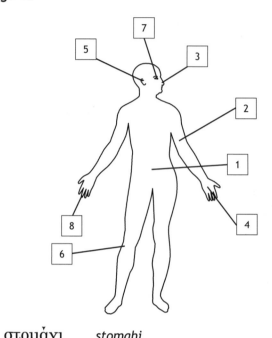

You should have also drawn pictures of:
leg; mouth; ear; nose; eye; hair

Page 41 (bottom)

κεφάλι	*kefali*
αυτί	*afti*
στομάχι	*stomahi*
μύτη	*miti*
βραχίονας	*vrahionas*
στόμα	*stoma*
μάτι	*mati*
πλάτη	*plati*

Page 42

1. στομάχι   *stomahi*
2. βραχίονας   *vrahionas*
3. μύτη   *miti*
4. χέρι   *heri*
5. αυτί   *afti*
6. πόδι   *poтні*
7. μάτι   *mati*
8. δάχτυλο   *тнаhtilo*

Page 43

ear	αυτί	*afti*
hair	μαλλιά	*malia*
hand	χέρι	*heri*
stomach	στομάχι	*stomahi*
arm	βραχίονας	*vrahionas*
back	πλάτη	*plati*
finger	δάχτυλο	*тнаhtilo*
leg	πόδι	*poтні*

8 USEFUL EXPRESSIONS

Page 45 (top)

great!	υπέροχα!
yes	ναι
yesterday	χθες
where?	πού;
today	σήμερα
here	εδώ
please	παρακαλώ
no	όχι

Page 45 (bottom)

εκεί	e<u>k</u>i
γειά	ya
αύριο	<u>a</u>vrio
αντίο	an<u>d</u>io
πόσο;	<u>p</u>oso?
ευχαριστώ	efhari<u>s</u>to
συγγνώμη	si<u>ghn</u>omi
υπέροχα!	iperoha!

Page 46

English word: please

Page 47

Page 48

yes	ναι	ne
hello	γειά	ya
no	όχι	<u>oh</u>i
sorry	συγγνώμη	see<u>ghn</u>omi
please	παρακαλώ	parakal<u>o</u>
there	εκεί	e<u>k</u>i
thank you	ευχαριστώ	efhari<u>s</u>to
tomorrow	αύριο	<u>a</u>vrio

● ROUND-UP

Page 49

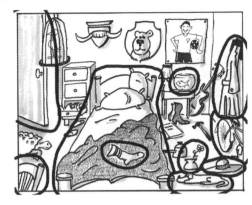

Page 50

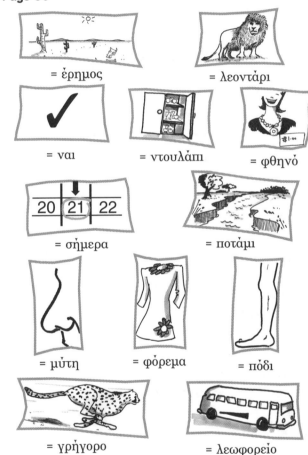

= έρημος = λεοντάρι

= ναι = ντουλάπι = φθηνό

= σήμερα = ποτάμι

= μύτη = φόρεμα = πόδι

= γρήγορο = λεωφορείο

Page 51

τραπέζι (Because it isn't an animal.)

τηλέφωνο (Because it isn't a means of transportation.)

αγρόκτημα (Because it isn't an item of clothing.)

δέντρο (Because it isn't connected with water.)

κινηματογράφος (Because it isn't a descriptive word.)

ψάρι (Because it lives in water/doesn't have legs.)

καναπές (Because it isn't a part of the body.)

παρακαλώ (Because it isn't an expression of time.)

κρεβάτι (Because you wouldn't find it in the kitchen.)

Page 52

Words that appear in the picture:

αθλητικό φανελλάκι
αυτοκίνητο
λουλούδι
παπούτσι
τρένο
μαϊμού
τηλεόραση
καρέκλα
ζώνη
σορτς

Page 53

sweater	πουλόβερ	poolover
lake	λίμνη	limni
thank you	ευχαριστώ	efharisto
bed	κρεβάτι	krevati
house	σπίτι	spiti
forest	δάσος	THasos
where?	πού;	poo?
heavy	βαρύ	vari

Page 54

English phrase: well done!

Page 55

σορτς	✔ (shade)
αθλητικό φανελλάκι	✘
πόρτα	✔ (handle)
γάτα	✘
καρέκλα	✔ (back)
ψάρι	✔ (direction)
κάλτσα	✔ (pattern)
σκύλος	✘

Page 56

refrigerator	ψυγείο
pants	παντελόνι
store	κατάστημα
school	σχολείο
river	ποτάμι
great!	υπέροχα!
small	μικρό
light	ελαφρύ
arm	βραχίονας
stomach	στομάχι
clean	καθαρό
horse	άλογο

Page 57

γειά	ya
χθες	hthes
φούρνος	foornos
κινηματογράφος	kinimatografos
ταξί	taksi
βουνό	voono
χωράφι	horafi
μεγάλο	meghalo
καινούργιο	kenooryo
πρόβατο	provato
δάχτυλο	THahtilo
ελέφαντας	elefandas

Page 58

Here are the English equivalents of the word, in order from START to FINISH:

eye	mati	ear	afti
cat	ghata	expensive	akrivo
taxi	taksi	hair	malia
sea	thalasa	house	spiti
no	ohi	duck	papia
here	eTHO	dirty	vromiko
door	porta	hand	heri
now	tora	heavy	vari
hill	lofos	tomorrow	avrio
old	palio	back	plati
rabbit	kooneli	leg	poTHi
slow	argho	yes	ne

υπολογιστὴς

ipologhi<u>stis</u>

παρἀθυρο

pa<u>ra</u>thiro

τραπἑζι

tra<u>pe</u>zi

ντουλἀπι

doo<u>la</u>pi

ψυγεἰο

psi<u>yi</u>o

καρἐκλα

ka<u>re</u>kla

καναπἑς

kana<u>pe</u>s

φοὑρνος

<u>foo</u>rnos

πὀρτα

<u>po</u>rta

κρεβἀτι

kre<u>va</u>ti

τηλἑφωνο

ti<u>le</u>fono

τηλεὀραση

tile<u>o</u>rasi

window	computer
cupboard	table
chair	refrigerator
stove	sofa
bed	door
television	telephone

ζώνη

zoni

επανωφόρι

epanofori

φούστα

foosta

καπέλο

kapelo

αθλητικό
φανελλάκι

athlitiko fanelaki

παπούτσι

papootsi

πουλόβερ

poolover

πουκάμισο

pookamiso

σορτς

sorts

κάλτσα

kaltsa

παντελόνι

pandeloni

φόρεμα

forema

coat	belt
hat	skirt
shoe	t-shirt
shirt	sweater
sock	shorts
dress	pants

σχολείο

sholio

αυτοκίνητο

aftokinito

δρόμος

THromos

κινηματογράφος

kinimatografos

ξενοδοχείο

ksenoTHohio

κατάστημα

katastima

ταξί

taksi

ποδήλατο

pothilato

εστιατόριο

estiatorio

λεωφορείο

leoforio

τρένο

treno

σπίτι

spiti

car	school
movie theater	road
store	hotel
bicycle	taxi
bus	restaurant
house	train

λὶμνη

limni

δᾰσος

THasos

λὸφος

lofos

θᾰλασσα

thalasa

βουνὸ

voono

δὲντρο

THendro

ἐρημος

erimos

λουλοὺδι

looloοΤΗi

γὲφυρα

yefira

ποτᾰμι

potami

αγρὸκτημα

aghroktima

χωρᾰφι

horafi

forest	lake
sea	hill
tree	mountain
flower	desert
river	bridge
field	farm

βαρὺ	ελαφρὺ
vari	*elafri*
μεγὰλο	μικρὸ
meghalo	*mikro*
παλιὸ	καινοὺργιο
palio	*kenooryo*
γρὴγορο	αργὸ
ghrighoro	*argho*
καθαρὸ	βρὼμικο
katharo	*vromiko*
φθηνὸ	ακριβὸ
fthino	*akrivo*

light	heavy
small	big
new	old
slow	fast
dirty	clean
expensive	inexpensive

πἄπια

papia

γἄτα

ghata

ποντἴκι

pondiki

αγελἄδα

ayelатна

κουνἔλι

kooneli

σκὔλος

skilos

ἄλογο

alogho

μαϊμοὔ

maimoo

λεοντἄρι

leondari

ψἄρι

psari

ελἔφαντας

elefandas

πρὄβατο

provato

| cat | duck |
| monkey | horse |

cat

duck

cow

mouse

dog

rabbit

monkey

horse

fish

lion

sheep

elephant

βραχἰονας	δἀχτυλο
vrahionas	*THahtilo*
κεφἀλι	στὀμα
kefali	*stoma*
αυτἰ	πὀδι
afti	*poTHi*
χἑρι	στομἀχι
heri	*stomahi*
μἀτι	μαλλιἀ
mati	*malia*
μὐτη	πλἀτη
miti	*plati*

finger	arm
mouth	head
leg	ear
stomach	hand
hair	eye
back	nose

8 USEFUL EXPRESSIONS

παρακαλώ *parakalo*	ευχαριστώ *efharisto*
ναι *ne*	όχι *ohi*
γειά *ya*	αντίο *andio*
χθες *hthes*	σήμερα *simera*
αύριο *avrio*	πού; *poo?*
εδώ *etho*	εκεί *eki*
συγγνώμη *sighnomi*	πόσο; *poso?*
υπέροχα! *iperoha!*	τώρα *tora*

thank you	please
no	yes
goodbye	hello
today	yesterday
where?	tomorrow
there	here
how much?	sorry!
now	great!